A Dangerous Heaven
Copyright © 2023 JoAngela Edwins

Original Cover Art by Brandon Mullis
Author Photo by Adam Houle

The font used is Brioche and Perpetua
The cover fonts are Brioche, Didot LT Pro Roman, and Lust Italic

All rights reserved. No duplication or reuse of any selection is allowed without the express written consent of the publisher.

Gnashing Teeth Publishing
242 East Main Street
Norman AR 71960

Printed in the United States of America

ISBN 979-8-9854833-9-0

Library of Congress Control Number 2023943371

Fiction: Poetry

Gnashing Teeth Publishing First Edition

Praise for A Dangerous Heaven

By searching inside words like "even" and "never" to find the name of Eve, the first poem in *A Dangerous Heaven* invites us to use language, the medium by which we receive sacred stories, to question and illuminate those stories. In this keenly contemplative collection, naming and other language acts, and words–mistaken or intended–become the vehicles by which Jo Angela Edwins' vivid figures build and rebuild stories of community and history, spirit and self. What kindles and compels in these poems is their fierce, generous lyric attention–to family, to the earth, to story and words for tenderness, violence, and terrible beauty, particularly in the lives of women, contemporary and Biblical. Edwins' meditative images consider the "wild electrical stretch" of a human body's craving, or the mystery of the luna moth, "what it means to be born / to a form so beautiful / the symmetry leaves / no space for a mouth, / no need to cry out." But these poems will cry out, because "sometimes we can do / no more in this dusky world than plead to air." They listen, too, anew for the voice of God, which may sound to Moses like "the hushed singing of our mothers." Their discoveries offer bright chances to see where beauty and grief meet, and to "declare the cotton / falling from cottonwood / a giving, not a leaving"–to re-name what needs re-naming, taking language into their own bold and wondrous hands.

Sally Rosen Kindred, author of *Where the Wolf*

In *A Dangerous Heaven*, Jo Angela Edwins walks us through a multi-layered grief process for accumulated wrongs and losses: historical, biblical, global, national, and personal. "It is your responsibility to grieve," one poem says, and this is not a command, but an acknowledgement. These poems don't look away from wounds, especially those of women, and they don't turn elsewhere for comfort, yet they leave me feeling seen and comforted. Everyone needs to read this book.

Katie Manning, author of *Hereverent* and *Tasty Other*

An intimate volume with cosmic reach, witty and compassionate, *A Dangerous Heaven* transports us through a wide range of emotions, carries us to lofty and surprising places which might be dangerous if we didn't have Jo Angela Edwins's sure hand to catch us, to place our feet firmly on home soil. Crafted to honor insight and emotion, these daring poems will keep us company over time, like trusted friends.

>Marilyn Kallet, author of 19 books, including
>*Even When We Sleep*, poetry from Black Widow Press

A Dangerous Heaven

Table of Contents

Eve	1
Magdalene	3
A Dangerous Heaven	4
A Student Spells "Abel" as "Able"	5
Walking around Furniture	7
Actias luna	9
Geophagy	10
This Year	11
Appellations	12
The Bedouin Wife	14
The Concept of Order	15
Children in Antique Photographs	17
MRI	18
The Last Wild Elephant Alive	19
Breaking News	20
An American Woman Steps inside an 800-Year-Old Church	21
Bathsheba	22
From Wire Reports	24
For Newtown, For Townville	26
The Children Have Stopped Crying	27
Broken Statues in Wartime	28
Distances	29
Like	30
Miniature Coffins	31
How It Feels to Be Bodiless	32

All Is Done	33
Postcard	35
The Way of Things	36
The Beauty of Stark Things	39
Death, A Rock Icon, and Sewage Pipes	41
December 19, 2016	43
Mary	46
The Mystery	47
Coordinates	48
A Failure of Seeing	50
Her Cap	51
Old Wives' Tale	52
A Woman Named Stanley	53
Craving	56
Walking on Eggshells	57
Wonder Woman at 90	58
That Hurt	59
When the Dog Bites	60
Mothers Build Stories	62
Leah, Rachel, Dinah	64
Clinging	66
Neighbors, 2017	68
Parents	69
Sick with Love	70
In Dreams	72
Harvest	73

Replenishing	74
Their Love Story	76
The Ceremony	77
Calhoun	80
Caim	81
Visitation	82
The Thought of Losing You	83
Elegy for Elegies	85
Further Reading	87
Acknowledgments	93
Personal Acknowledgements	95
About the Author	99

EVE

How many words
contain her name—
even, as if
she had an even
chance. *Prevent*,
as if her sin
weren't pre-ordained.
Of course, *every*,
as she was the mother
of it all, dark
and light, yes,
even the serpent,
her writhing child,
the birth of her
undoing. Who
can blame her, not
trusting the men, the
father who commands
without explanation,
the mate who complains
of the pain she left
in his robbed breast?
The prophet had him
sounding thankful, proof
the prophet thought
himself a man.
Any wonder she
identified
with a thing soon to be
forced to crawl
each day on its belly?

But that's not right.
She proved strong, as are all
things built of bone.
How else explain
her choice to leave
paradise (make no
mistake), to bring
a beautifully flawed
world into being?
Who else but this
stiff-backed woman,
caught in the midst of
both never and forever?

MAGDALENE

She knew the men wouldn't believe her.
As she ran to find them, she imagined
their feet pounding away all trace
of her backwards footprints. Their eyes must see
the empty tomb for themselves.
She couldn't blame them. She would want
herself to be witness too,
even to absence. Stories are powerful
and best told in first-person.
And they would not see what she saw,
the man-god they each loved
with their weak human hearts, speaking to her
in a risen glory so quiet
it stilled the wind. Then she wondered
if the men with their wine-stained lips
and furtive denials had eclipsed Eve's curse,
if a woman might be born again a cornerstone.
But no. Beneath it all, she understood
the men would return, redeemed.
Even Thomas, awash in disbelief,
would be asked to plunge his hands in God's wounds.
She was told not to touch, but she needed
no such invitation anyway.
Blood was her intimate.
She recognized the gash and crush
of violent possession. She was a stranger
to the frozen landscapes of doubt.

A Dangerous Heaven

It was her safe heaven.

— a student's misspelling

Was she happy to escape it,
such perilous perfection,
a daredevilish nirvana,
pandemonic peace?

Was there a risk in leaving?
Was she as likely to land
in any hell as in safe heaven?
Would safe hell have been worse?
Or are they merely different labels
for the same uneven terrain?

Hence the squabbles for dominion
between the fallen angel named Lucifer
and the risen savior who declared himself
the Light of the World.

A Student Spells "Abel" as "Able"

and I cannot help myself, I must
imagine poor Abel as able
to defend himself, perhaps to whip
Cain with the cane we mostly come to
lean on in time, beating backwards
not only the murderer within us but also
our gradual decline towards death, our succumbing
to the putrefaction of original sin—
the strength in evil, the weakness in good, twin
objects of our wildest loathings.

Old preachers in their manly self-righteousness
would love for us to believe Eve's craving
for tart fruits doomed us all, but truth be told,
those sad brothers were the first tipsy domino.
Abel's blood spills into desert sand,
and it trickles through millennia to robber barons,
dope runners, cock fighters, husbands
and wives, and children in close school desks
who cheat without thinking twice.
This is what it comes to, poor Abel, your blood:
a girl stealing paperbacks from dime stores,
a boy throwing stones at dirty windows.

Ask Jesus, your sad-faced descendant:
the only worse thing than dying to save them
is dying to make them in need of a savior.
As if you had a choice in the matter.
As if none of us know the real culprit in it all,
his head resting in clouds he called into being,
his bodiless body stretched out on a bed

softer than forgiveness, as wide as the land
where the rock in your brother's hand fell.

Walking around Furniture

We learn the pathways to navigate our spaces
filled with things to help us live our lives,
the tables that hold our food and pens and papers,
the chairs that hold us,
the lamps that light these paths when night falls.
We fear emptiness
more than the shabbiest of things we use
to steady our footing in this physical world,
things that collect the particles of us
that die before we do, and we don't mind,
say these coatings prove our rooms are lived in,
before we wipe them away.

And there is the bed that, perhaps, we share.
And there is in the next room perhaps a crib.

And perhaps if we know the story then sometimes
we think of the Chinese who die alone and childless,
no one to love their souls enough
to offer them food in the afterlife,
sweet seared fish, golden loaves of bread,
and so they wander, stepping gingerly around
other ghosts with loved ones and full bellies.

And so they scream,
slapping dishes from the shelves, slamming doors,
splintering floor planks, making a mess
of a house no longer tied to their name,
a name that fades like ink in rain.

The tenants run, scared mice before a flood,
never to return. Glass-splattered floors
are soaked with the invisible
blood of troubled spirits' weary,
lacerated feet. This is the story
we think of, if we know it. If we think

long enough, we understand that we know it.
So we try not to think. Instead, we plump pillows,
build bookshelves, drop flowers in vases,
hug our children, if we have them.
Sing songs to ourselves, softly, if we don't.

ACTIAS LUNA

What it means to be born
to a form so beautiful
the symmetry leaves
no space for a mouth,
no need to cry out
to this world, no need
to eat. Only drive
to stretch wings
and spill young
of this same florid
beauty, then
die in the night,
to make room.

Geophagy

We quote scripture—
"dust to dust"—and we
quote the "they"
in "They say," as in
"They say you are
what you eat." So we
swallow the earth's
whiteboned ash
of itself, the ground breaking
down like a stiff corpse
burned by summers,
marching towards eternity
and rising inside us, a bird
of wind and flame and mist,
elemental as we are, winging
towards the heaven that teaches us
to cast off earthly things, and yet
who can cast off what
we fail to take in?
No sin in this, devouring
what the good lord animated
with a wave and a word,
the ribs of Adam built
with the silt of the Tigris.
The clay beneath your feet
is anything but dead. Listen.
It sings to you. Listen.
It whispers, *This, my*
body. Take it,
and eat.

This Year

The brothers at the fraternity house decided
to smear a blow-up doll with scarlet paint
and leave it in the yard, head bowed, legs splayed,
a cheap Halloween decoration.

Four women were found murdered in this small city
in three months. A grandmother who sang in church,
hunched in a ditch. Two women, cousins,
sunken in shallow graves behind
their killer's ramshackle house.
Another woman, shrouded in an urban field
overgrown with kudzu. Workers cleaning
the wide lot smelled what they thought was a dead
stray dog for days and said nothing, only hacked
with greater care the nearer they came to the corner
that hid what made them afraid.

    In another
county, a woman, home from communion,
discovered her pug, a puppy, her first pet,
roasted in an oven, the door wedged shut
with her grandmother's parson's chair.

              And people wonder still
why we tell sad women's stories.
We listen to such questions. We light candles.
Put on a pot of tea. Pull dark bread
from the cupboards. Ask the people to sit down.

APPELLATIONS

In the quiet of a kitchen table,
in the morning, before another creature
in the house is stirring, or else the loud
beat of radio, motor, jackhammer, siren
and city traffic, or the in-between of
an office desk or bank line or lunch counter,
names of things come to you, the sounds
of words you can't swear to the meaning of
sometimes ringing in your ears like forgotten
favorite songs you never quite learned the lyrics to
but loved the melodies, words that mean
good things and bad, words like *amaryllis,*
tarantella, tachycardia, monsoon,
elderberry, agapanthus, arpeggio,
and soon enough come nations, towns, rivers,
Tajikistan, Nacogdoches, Chattahoochee,
and animals in familiar foreignness—
armadillo, koala, cephalopod,
and you wonder where the words came from,
and you wonder sometimes where they go
when people stop using them, words like *betimes,*
doxy, grimalkin, habiliment, and soon
enough you're considering silence, that valuable
terror, that space between words on the page,
or worse yet, the blankness after the final
period, by which of course you mean *death*
without saying *death* to yourself (how did things
turn this dark over words?), and you being you,
which is to say you being human, being worried
about what it means to be alive, you wonder
as humans often must what death will feel like,

when it will come, what happens to you after,
and yes, go on, wonder, we can't help ourselves—
who will be there to mourn you? What words will they say?

The Bedouin Wife

Wherever they settled, she dreamt the place she left
still held the things she needed most—the spoon
she fed her sons with buried in a dune,
as if the earth demanded such cruel theft,

or in the ashes of the rubbish heap
the rings her husband gave her when they wed.
Around her fingers bits of fraying thread
replaced the trust she had no hope to keep.

Some nights, she watched herself meandering back
to places other tribes had claimed, to sift
through dust and twigs for some forgotten gift
long since deposited in a peddler's pack.

Some nights, she became the thing they threw away,
walking old borders, searching distant haze
in case she was missed, until the press of days
convinced her of the hell it means to stay.

And when she woke those nights, she understood
that no more sleep would come. Instead, the thrill
of knowing her body to be awake and still
enough to hear the movement of her blood.

The Concept of Order

As a species, humans
live their lives in degrees
of alarm. Mostly, for most
of us, there isn't much.
The world spins exactly
as we have come to expect it,
and caught wherever
we are, sleepy plain
or teetering city, our psyches
adjust to whatever
routine keeps us relatively
free from harm. Introduce
imminent disaster,
and rules crumble.
Consider the freeway
when a hurricane hovers
off the coast: suddenly
all lanes creep inland.
A library on fire
is no place for whispers.
Such inversions
are just as they should be.
But how explain panic
without cause? The aging
machinist who slings
insults at the young
immigrant, or,
much more dire,
the scared cop who fires
on the kid jogging home
from the store with nothing

on his person but candy
and spare change. At least,
if we put our minds to it,
we might unearth the wicked
fear beneath such frailties.
But what about this:
workers in their pressed clothes
that bright September day
who had felt the impact
of the 767
against glass and steel
so many stories up
and took time to gather files,
pack briefcases, shut down
slow computers, as if
it were 5 o'clock on any
given weekday, not the dawn
of Armageddon, not a slide
to an age of search
and seizure, not—
if they could not hurry
down too many flights of stairs—
the last day of their lives.
Or was it just that?
A calm capitulation
to the inevitable silence.
If I must go, at least
let me build this modest shrine
to the concept of order:
pens corralled in a cup,
mugs washed and dried and shelved,
papers straightened and stacked neatly
before the rendering to ash.

Children in Antique Photographs

so often seem frightened,
propped up, rigid as mailboxes,
in front of serious adults,
or leaning with friends, half-bent
in a stance like a track runner's,
alert to the sound of the gun, and
off they'll dart. Those of certain classes
stand wrapped like sad sausages
in taffeta or tweed. Too many of the rest
wear suffering on their faded sleeves,
stained collars, worn pockets,
their faces as hopeless as the packed clay
leading to their closed doors.
Nearly all, no matter how smooth or smeared
their skin, have hair combed neatly, or curled,
a testament to some concerned adult's
notion of the permanence of pictures,
as if brush and camera
might erase every blemish,
and today, of course, the camera can,
but not so then. Not so when
the earth understood what it means to be
awash in shades of gray,
no orange, no red-skinned apple
shimmering in lemon sunlight,
nothing but shadow where often, today,
a flash might convince us of brightness.

MRI

Cocooned in this plastic womb,
you are a shivering chrysalis
struggling to stay still as the dead
silicone surrounding you, and somewhere
outside this insulated world there thrums
elevator music, the cartoon dreams
it sings drowned out at last
by that hammering drone reminding you
we are all being pounded to dust
in the end. Sometimes a tinny
voice asks how you do. You cough,
say "fine," then the pounding
resumes, all in valiant effort
to figure what went wrong. Lying here,
stripped of rings and bracelets and brassiere,
you count the filigrees on the one strip
of wallpaper you see, then count the lights
that float behind shut eyelids, then count
the chances you've missed year by year.
Beyond shut doors, people are doing things
you've done before without thinking—
pumping gas, counting change, telling someone
whose face they can't see to have a nice day.
In here you think of someone you love.
In here you wonder what that person felt
the last time he heard you speak his name.

The Last Wild Elephant Alive

will munch bamboo alone
on a remote savanna, uneasy
to be herdless, and she will wonder
(I guess a *she*, because the smallest
are often killed last) where her family
disappeared to, and she will remember
(because it isn't a lie; elephants do remember)
every scarred contour of the trunks of her brothers
and sisters and mates and children shattered
by a blast her weak eyes might barely see
but her wide ears will hear all too well.

What I say here is mostly true, but know this:
the last wild elephant alive will not
have time to chew bamboo and stand
puzzled at her gargantuan loneliness.
The gun that fells the rest of her kind
will slaughter her too, for sport if not
for tusk. Humans adore the carbon
scent of rapid-fire extinction, humans
with their small half-heart-shaped ears
that hear the report of the rifle,
that hear the deep groan of a majestic thing
losing the last of its breath, and remain
unmoved. Perhaps these same humans feel
a quiver in their feet at the trembling ground
that quakes when wild pachyderms fall.
Soon enough they forget what shakes them.

Breaking News

Children die in shooting spree.
Carcinogens found in food supply.
World leaders disagree.

Hundreds of frightened civilians flee
troops on ground, war planes in sky.
Children die in shooting spree.

Polar melt swells every sea.
Fuel prices climb to record high.
World leaders disagree.

Protesters make impassioned plea.
Students shout while parents cry.
Children die in shooting spree.

Big business adds another fee.
Candidate caught in another lie.
World leaders disagree.

Humanity's gone refugee.
No one has an alibi.
Children die in shooting spree.
World leaders disagree.

An American Woman Steps Inside an 800-Year-Old Church

I feel like an interloper.
I feel like a baby
not old enough for baptism,
or worse, like a minor demon,
my evil mild as an ant bite.
The air smells of beeswax
and moldering Latin.
I do not dip my fingers
in chalky holy water.
I do not genuflect
at prescribed points, I do not
drape lacy kerchiefs over
my bared head. I mean no
disrespect when I sit
in a pew not carved for me
to find a lower angle
from which to snap a picture
of the glorious, burnished Christ
on an age-blackened cross.
Music drifts from somewhere.
In another pew, a couple speaks
to each other in quiet French.
The walls around us are thick as history,
as oceans, as spilled blood.
Tears gather in my eyes
for no clear reason.
I stand to leave. The Christ
above me says nothing.

Bathsheba

How you can tell the story was told by men:
the tragic hero is King David, the favorite
of the God they imagined to be a man
in their own image. And David took what he wanted,
the privilege of men and of kings. He stood
upon a balcony and watched her bathe.
He did not turn away. He did not question
the firmness of his gaze. Instead, he plotted
and commanded, another privilege
of men and of kings.

                    Pay attention: see how easily
he overtakes the story.

But how could he not? Her voice, like her body,
was not her own. Unlike her body, her voice was a thing
no man wished to touch or understand,
though it spoke an ancient language,
the essence of the breath in his lungs.

Perhaps she consented. Perhaps she looked up
from her spot of earth and saw the king,
a thing the world tells us is beautiful. Perhaps
she truly thought him beautiful. If he can claim
what is beautiful as his own, why not she?

More likely she did not. More likely she recognized
that his power, a mad dog that can turn a lick of love
to teeth at the throat in an instant, could destroy her
quickly as the warrior's spear to her husband's breast.

How unexpected that this time the king feels the thousand
stings of the arrows of his errant ways, sons gone wild
with desire, for a sister, for vengeance, for the father's
concubines raped in the streets, for the father's throne.
How many bled in the name of their greed.

But she suffered too: her first child dead, and all
the king could do was name the loss his punishment,
eat warm bread when he knew his prayers held no sway
over the issue. All the while, her grief, no doubt,
was deeper than the deadest sea.

She was destined to bear for him again
a son who would sing hymns to lust,
hymns men would declare a perfumed letter
in the heavy word of God. And that son too
would become a hungry king.

Was it because David was God's
chosen father of the savior of the world
that the tale of his punishment
overshadows her silenced pain?

Or is that silence the closest thing
the scribbling men who played God with story
could offer as sympathy, as justice, in a world
that built our own, and was at least as blind?

FROM WIRE REPORTS

The four-sentence story
in the small-town, U.S. paper
made no mention of an aftermath.

In fact, the story itself
was told the way it almost happened:
the first two sentences,
paragraphs to themselves,
described the spectacle of bombers
dropping scores of paper cranes
over Thailand's southern provinces,
strange births, fragile promises
that peace will burst from war.

In Bangkok, so many miles
away, the Prime Minister
called the gesture a success,
hailed the cranes as bright reminders
that the Muslims of the south
were Thais as much as he, bound
to northern countrymen
in peace and in care.

"The campaign didn't stop the violence,"
the final paragraph began.
Those who read that far
while carpooling to work
or eating café breakfasts
in their disquieted mind's eye
imagined what would have been
the deafening blow

of the 22-pound bomb
dismantled safely before detonation
on a road crowded with children
waiting to glean tiny cranes falling
like petals, like snow, like bread from a heaven
almost forgotten,
still not quite sure of itself.

For Newtown, For Townville

In a cinderblock room
painted the colors
of spring gardens, of cartoons,
the children sway in time
to a song they sing
about rainbows. Yellow suns,
blue skies, green grass,
red cherries. There is
no verse about the golden
brass of a shell casing,
the black of a flak jacket,
the steel gray barrel
in the hands of the boy
eight or ten years their senior,
so sick he can't swallow,
so he kills instead.
One. Two. Three. Four.
His mind races through
a dark lesson on arithmetic
and indifference. The blood
that drums through his shriveling
heart is no duller
than a kindergartner's.
In the end, the white floor
is stained a dusky hue
between cherries and grief.
The clock on the wall
ticks its usual rhythm,
counting seconds until
it happens again.

The Children Have Stopped Crying

"Aleppo is a place where the children have stopped crying."
              - Channel 4 online video of victims of repeated Syrian and Russian
                                                bombing, December 2016

But the only adult
still alive in the family
cannot stop wailing
at the death of her daughter,
and the teenage neighbor
caught in between
hospital doorframes
will not let go
of the swaddled corpse
of his one-month-old brother.

And the children's faces,
grayed by the dust
of smithereened buildings,
turn towards and away from
the camera, their eyes
blank as the sky once
the planes have disappeared.

Their hands, baby-fatted
and bloodied, fold politely
in their laps. They are
waiting for a doctor
to dress their wounds.
They are waiting for their aunt
to stop moaning. They are
waiting for someone
to tell them exactly
what to do now.

Broken Statues in Wartime

Gray, they fade grayer
beneath this mustard sun.
Here feet, there fingers,
cracked eyes, lopped ears,
jagged folds of robe.
Dust of palm, hair, wings, any
man's guess. They can wound
if you touch them ungloved.
Step away. Someone who knows
should bring shovels, a bag,
gather the rubble, cart it away
before someone else sees it—
a young parent, a child—
someone who can't hold the pain.

DISTANCES

June 2008

The summer my sister could not walk,
I slept uneasy in a tarnished brass bed
in the room beside hers, the door ajar
in case she called out. Two houses down
my father, still nervous in his old age,
drank tall cans of beer and forgot
to eat his meals. Almost a mile away,
the state ripped pines from their roots and scored
earth down to clay to stretch a highway,
named for a golf hero, in sweeping arcs
across two county lines. Sixty-four miles
in another direction, the thin-faced governor
signed into law a bill declaring indigo
the state's official color, then refused
to sign bills giving children of the poor
free visits to doctors and dentists. Five states away
rivers hemorrhaged from rain, submerging hospitals,
churches, cemeteries, while farther west,
fires blackened precarious canyon homes
and stands of giant redwood. Across the ocean,
women and men mourned the only children
the nation allowed them to have, buried beneath
the ruins of an earthquake-ravaged school, while
millions of miles above them, the sun glowered
one year hotter, undiminished by
the earth-bound's desperate grasp for energy.

Like

Not it,
but akin.
Not the dragon;
its reflection,
the ghost
in the glass.
Not the heady
luxury
of the open
gardenia,
but its bottled
perfume
suffusing
the room.
Not your face,
expressions
shimmering
like moonlight
on water.
Only this
photograph—
colder, flatter—
unable to answer
no matter
how often
I whisper
your name.

Miniature Coffins

Despite intense outcry from the medical community and reproductive rights advocates, the state [of Texas] will prohibit hospitals, abortion clinics and other health care facilities from disposing of fetal remains in sanitary landfills, instead allowing only cremation or burial of all remains — regardless of the period of gestation.
                              -The Texas Tribune, *November 28, 2016*

You have a vagina; you contain a womb.
It is your responsibility to grieve, to bear
the burden of your body's sad lack to its tomb.

A lily gone sick before it can bloom
need only fall to earth and crumble there,
but you have a vagina. You contain a womb,

a small, sullied, sanctified room
in which grows a microscopic heir
to Adam's sin, a child bound for the tomb

sooner or later--a wisp, a soul, a plume
in its father's distant cap, one he may not wish to wear.
But he touched your vagina. He seeded your womb,

and the sorrow is yours now. You shouldn't presume
to manage your own losses. The state takes great care
of its citizenry, from uterus to tomb.

Don't bother to question how to bury or exhume
a casketed embryo, much less why or where.
You have a vagina; you contain a womb.
You are an empty vessel. You are a plundered tomb.

How It Feels to Be Bodiless

So often in the center of a street
a single shoe—frayed laces, fractured heel—
lies sad and inert as a dead bird,
as if he too fell from the sky and waits
like a fool for the other to drop,
but she doesn't. Somewhere in the heavens
she dances her indie hop jauntily,
happy perhaps that her bumble-tongued mate
took at last that lonely flying leap,
lost himself in rubber-wheeled traffic,
the perfect place to bare his step-worn soul.
No one wants him now.
He will be battered by everything, elements,
Hondas, Harleys, harried pedestrians
who kick him from underfoot to save themselves
from falling in his place. He will discover
what it means to lie in the gutter.
He will, like all of us someday, understand
how it feels to be bodiless forever,
a vessel for nothing, a thing without use—
that freedom, that terrible freedom.

All Is Done

Lockdown, lockdown, lock the door
Shut the lights off, say no more.

Go behind the desks and hide
Wait until it's safe inside.

Lockdown, lockdown, all is done.
Now it's time to have some fun!

> \- Nursery rhyme taught to Massachusetts schoolchildren about active shooter lockdowns (Source: The Boston Globe, June 7, 2018)

Mother Goose conjures
tame horrors at worst:

cracked eggs, spiders,
children tumbling down hills.

Jack and Jill keep getting up
to climb those hills again,

Miss Muffet never loses her taste
for curds and whey,

and always some adult voice achieves
what all the king's men can't, even if

Humpty Dumpty is destined
to fall again. And again.

But this song is a lie. Too many
flesh-and-blood children

learn too quickly the meanings
of flesh and of blood, forget

the sugar-coated definition
of fun. Indeed, now, all is done.

Rhyme and rhythm will not fit
these pieces back together.

Stilled bodies won't rise
to mount again a soft, green hill.

In this poison-apple world,
all the king's men

never learn their lessons.
They keep building walls

and prop more children atop them,
so many glass bottles,

so many shattered hearts.

POSTCARD

A man in a downstairs apartment moves
furniture from his patio to an old Chevy van.
He wears blue jeans and stained leather gloves.
His steps are sure and solid. A focused man.
Fresh from committee fights and your last goodbye,
I envy his smooth efficiency.
He carries a chair across concrete, and I
could measure what he's done.
                                    Soon he is free
to close all doors and leave. Simple as that,
I want to believe, though each pore of me senses
I don't know the story of what makes him go:
a father's illness, a lost job, a lover's spat.
Gaze as we might through curtains, over fences,
who can trace the gap between *see* and *know*?

The Way of Things

Once my friend and I stood
before an empty cage
at the state's biggest zoo,
looking vainly for the creatures
that should have been there.
She turned to the sign
on the cage, then turned
to me. "Li-MOORS.
What the hell are
li-MOORS?" "Lemurs,"
I said. She laughed
a genuine laugh at herself.
"What the fuck"—my friend
likes to curse, and I love her
for it—"What the fuck
is wrong with me?"
All afternoon, when
conversation lulled, we'd
whisper "Li-MOOR"
to each other, and cackle.

Another time, in a shore-side
city, we sat
in a diner frequented
by colorful locals—
a truck driver in sunglasses
and a sad toupee,
a mime in full costume,
an old man who talked
to an invisible dog.
Our friendly waiter

told us their stories, then
gave us a check
he'd forgotten to split.
"I'll split it," I said,
then messed up the math,
and it took my friend twenty minutes
to convince me I'd forgotten
to carry a one.

"We all do dumb things,"
an insurance commercial
used to remind us
on mindless TV.
Our brains are beautiful
disasters, the way
they persuade us we've every
right to believe
we're right about everything
most of the time, then
tripping us faster
than the rickety heel
on a cheap pair of pumps.

This is the way of things.

The mind brilliant enough
to paint imaginary faces
on a body, then take it
to a park, where it dances
in a farce of entrapment
in invisible prisons
to generate laughter, to
make us think twice
about what being human

really means, is the mind
that thinks it a brilliant
idea to steal creatures
from their natural jungles
then cart them like vegetables
to cities with cages
that lock them inside
to be watched by the likes
of themselves, only louder,
only smarter perhaps—
only smarter, if we measure
smarts by our faulty,
sometimes logical brains
and not by our much more
glorious, if often
hardened, or broken,
mad, beating hearts.

The Beauty of Stark Things

A celebration of the plain
or the natural, however
full of emptiness
a thing might be.

The rusted hinge gone green,
marsh reeds bleached blond
in winter, the grayed feather and bone
of the hawk, dead and plundered
on the highway's edge.

Inching closer towards the human...

There. At a table in a quiet café,
a woman sits alone. Sometimes
she gazes at a spoon or doorknob so long
her mind must be elsewhere.
Or not. Perhaps the sheen
of industrial light on cheap metal
captivates. She wouldn't be
the first. Either way, look at her, not
what she looks at. Notice
the face, no longer young, so stiff with thought
you cannot help but imagine pain,
and somewhere, there is no doubt
pain. Yes, look at the face,
pinched a bit now, eyes squinted,
lips cracked, not what this muddied
world would call beautiful. Still
you know it is beautiful, as beautiful
as fire or flood, as beautiful as

a stopped heart, beautiful like all of us,
terrible, beautiful, so terribly beautiful.

Death, a Rock Icon, and Sewage Pipes

The day I found out David Bowie had died,
a plumber dug a pipe from my back yard,
showed me where it had rusted out, declared
it the least of my worries.
I know he referred only to plumbing,
but he was right. My head had been throbbing
for three days, my sister was paying
money from her dwindling retirement to stay
in a nursing home until, if we were lucky,
she'd be able to stand again, while one cousin
to the north of us was alone and weakening
from a stomach that would not stay still,
and two others, closer, battled cancer, one of whom
lay in a hospital bed, the third time in six weeks,
her lungs riddled with clots, her mind shivering with fear
of what would happen to the ones she loved most
were she to die. Our parents were already dead.

The plumber, of course, knew none of this,
nor did I know if he knew David Bowie—
a man whose insistence on slapping the world
off-kilter, on flipping from starman to Goblin King
demanded respect—had died a common
death the night before. I didn't mourn
for this man I knew little of and had never met,
as many of my friends mourned, but I understood
the need to grieve an energy, an artistry lost.
My mind went anyway to the powdered face
and spiked hair I'd seen on black-and-white TV
when I was a child, his alien features
and trembling voice odd forces, frightening

in a childhood already frightened enough.
I can't imagine seeing him then in color.

Weeks before I called the plumber, I'd read the story
of a woman who, when thirteen, became, she said,
Bowie's willing lover, as if a child of thirteen
has a choice in the matter. Perhaps my childish
fear was justified. There is no rule
which dictates genius need be meek or moral;
in fact, too many geniuses have proven
fragile as the pipe in the plumber's hands.

How much can be paid for with reinvention?
Not enough, I think, and still I imagine
the ash of our bodies blows in time to settle
to earth to feed small roots, stems growing from white
to green to rainbow, the colors of Bowie's wild mind.
Beauty and terror lie close in beds of change.

The plumber emerged from under the house—
skin and shirt grayed by pale clay—and I
was tempted to name him Lazarus (although
his name was Jason), to lose the moment imagining
him, my leashed dog, a staring neighbor, myself,
all of us leaping from dark holes in the earth,
our eyes bandaged and buttoned, unwilling to see
the messes still growing behind us when we rise,
still roiling in the atmosphere, a band of shining blow flies
and the relentless thump-thump of electrified drums.

December 19, 2016

In South Carolina, a cold rain,
not quite snow,
which would be strange
this early, this far south,
and farther north, the land
is frozen, although everywhere
the world is burning.

In Aleppo,
children line up
to receive a free toy
from a kind man
who may, like them,
die at any moment.
No jolly elf
with an avuncular beard,
he is a person
doing a wonderfully simple
thing. He is a person
who no doubt, at some point,
has hurt someone
past forgiveness.
No one, not even he,
thinks about that now.

In Ankara,
a man gone mad
from the carnage adds
to the carnage, shoots
the Russian ambassador,
screams revenge while

waving his pistol, and
photographers gathered
in an antiseptic gallery
for a photography exhibit
fail to duck. Instead, they do
what they are there to celebrate.
Pictures wash the internet
with stylized horror,
everyone wondering
at each crisp-captured image,
asking if it's real, if it's
a hoax, if it's a postmodern
drama. It's real. The gunman
soon enough is killed too.
Someone whispers somewhere,
"This is the way
world wars start."

In American state capitals,
protestors recalling
other world wars
gather with homemade signs,
with rainbow sweaters,
with quivering hearts,
begging electors
not to enshrine
a reality TV star
who sings to our wildest
hatreds as leader
of what some call the free
world. It has never been free.
The marchers ascend
marble steps in some states
in droves, in most states

in clusters that would barely
fill a bus. They might be
carolers singing
of refugees in the cold,
starlit desert. Men in suits
file past them, never turning
in their direction. Of course,
the electors do not listen.
The world is spinning
to the pedaling of those
too mindless to follow
the rhythm of symphonies.

And still
it is December,
two days before solstice.
In places, clouds hide
the waning gibbous
moon. In places, that moon
pours down its diminishing
light. Either way, the sky
behind it is as dark as
the history we are destined
to repeat, should we remember
or should we forget.

MARY

In Renaissance paintings she holds the child
like a porcelain doll. She sits surrounded
by animals and men, having given birth
in a stable, and she isn't the least
afraid. Sometimes artists build strange worlds
of meticulous Technicolor order.

She did not ask for this. She did not demand
that her statue mark every cathedral door
like cartoon faces on neon signs
outside chain restaurants. She had
in youth a mind of her own, a face of her own,
until an angel tossed pebbles at her window.

Now her name means nothing more than "mother."
It has lost its ancient thunder, the roar of the seas.
She is the low lullaby that followed
the howl of parturition that, wondrous, followed
the veiled silence of virginity.
What is left but the slow moan of grief?

No, nothing more than a marbled pietà,
the pierced and broken body of the son
draped across her arms, because the need
to carry never ends. Underneath
his wilted flesh, her bloodied robe, there rises
the breath she gave him once, and will again.

The Mystery

I hear of someone I barely know or don't know
dying young and suddenly, and I cannot help it,
I wonder how. Does everyone wonder how?
Do others shrug it off and go about
their business of pretending it would never
happen to them or someone they love, sweeping
leaves off the porch, writing the same dull checks
to utility companies, washing the same chipped plates
in gray dishwater? Perhaps they do. I know
it isn't commonplace to hold your gaze
on strangers' faces in newspapers, on lit screens,
and wonder what they thought the moment before
the chest pain, the tire skid, the trip and fall,
the bullet strike, and then to wonder which
fatality, futility, befell them,
as if the knowing were an abstract charm,
an invisible amulet against disaster,
whatever the disaster. And for whom
would the charm work? Yourself? Someone you love?
And if so, who? There we are again, the wonder
multiplying, like ripples in a pond
a child dropped a stone into, a lovely
stone that glittered in sunlight like a jewel,
a stone she didn't mean to drop, a stone
whose sinking she watched until it disappeared
into the darkness, that second before she missed it
enough to forget everything else, and dive.

COORDINATES

Some nights when the house was mostly quiet
and my father could find no games on TV,
he would sit in his chair in the den, the only light
the dim one at his elbow, and read maps
in a yellow-paged atlas bought for my sisters
a decade before, when they were in high school
and he was busy building houses—plumb corners
and squared joists constructing a sudden order
he craved but could not live by. How he loved
the precision of the straight line, the mystery
of the crooked. And so he sat for hours
tracing with thick fingers borders between
Russia and Mongolia, Chile and Argentina,
California and Oregon and a rolling ocean
he would never see. Some dividing lines
he knew quite well, the strange ridges he trudged
between Italy and Yugoslavia
at the end of a distant war, the doorways crossed
in his own war-weary home, the hill he climbed
to see his aging mother in the space
she shared once with his father, now long dead.
Sometimes, if the mood struck him, he would try
to speak the names of cities he knew nothing
about, and his eager tongue—taxed enough
to say long words in his own twangy language—
tripped on umlauts, tilds, and clumsy English
approximations of foreign alphabets.
"Byoonis Airs," I would hear him say
from my room at the top of the stairs. "Shang-Hey.
"Care-a-cass, Vy-inn-ah."
As the young do, I would laugh in his face
whenever he misspoke in conversation
what I always knew I knew better. I had not studied
carefully the borderlines between
jest and cruelty, the rough terrain of love.
Now I study maps on a computer screen

and think of this man—no stranger to his own
thunderings of meanness, but mostly a quiet spirit
content to learn what was offered him—sitting alone
as the evening aged, his eyes following rivers,
their sudden falls and gentle bends, to oceans
that kept grand continents apart but carried in ripples
small particles from this green land to that.

A Failure of Seeing

Ugliness is just a failure of seeing.

— Matt Haig

My mother loved babies,
held them with ease in her wide hands,
laughed, sang to them,
spoke in silly voices,
did all the foolish things people do
around genuine innocence.
Sometimes, when the visitors were gone,
the house mostly quiet again,
she would smile and say with no cruelty,
"That baby is so ugly he's cute!"
We knew just what she meant, the way
the off-center can be beautiful,
the way the scar proves the bearer
has a worthwhile story to tell,
the way the bruise-black funnel cloud swirls,
its irregular cone sleek and terrible
as a thousand tigers. Call it paradox,
call it sublime, call it the allure
of the alien, knowing nothing is alien.
The pulse of every particle,
however fair or plain, beats
in our own veins, where even blood—
a kingly crimson when spilling before us—
paints the walls of its airless tunnel
a shivery, sickly blue.

Her Cap

is ivory nylon and covers her head.
That's all. She does not wear it to cook or clean
or tend to the sick or the dead,
the work she did before. The band is thin
but clings to skin like perspiration.
Sewn in layers, it gives the illusion of hair.
It gathers in front for decoration
in a tightly wound rosette the color of air
and the shape, I imagine, of her subtle disease
in its solidness and swell and groove,
the thing her doctors call a condition, to ease
the weight on her chest which, unlike her cap,
                                        she did not put on
                                        and cannot remove.

Old Wives' Tale

With a kitchen knife I nicked my thumb
the night you left. But I want you to know
I washed it, wrapped it, kept going.

I peeled potatoes, freshly dug and smelling of rain,
chopped carrots, onions, tomatoes,
scraped Silver Queen from the cob
into the wide pot warming on the stove.
Like my mothers before me,
I gathered the ingredients, spiced and stirred,
and when the time came to let the stew simmer
uninterrupted, I sat and sipped tea,
falcon-eyed, watching the pot build its heat,
proving one old story, at least, untrue.

When at last my supper was ready,
I ladled thick liquid the color of blood
into a bowl deep as fists,
and when the tall shaker I never used fell,
salt spilled in tiny tracks, whitening the tablecloth.
With a folded napkin I wiped the fine grains
into my cupped hand and tossed them
first over the left shoulder, then over the right,
not, as they say, for good luck, but to keep
such stuff away from fresh wounds.

I finished my supper, down to the last spoonful,
and that night I slept like deep roots in winter
conjuring the colors of spring.

A Woman Named Stanley

In a 1970s game show,
a woman named Stanley
wins about $6,000,
which is worth, with inflation,
about $35,000 as of
the writing of this poem.

She explains that her mother
loved Bette Davis, who played
a woman named Stanley
in a film aptly titled
In This Our Life.

Stanley plays against
men and women, but among
her many challengers
are women named Fil and Gary.
(Fil was called Fil because
a boyfriend couldn't pronounce
her name, which was "Felicit,"
a name that means *happiness*.)

Stanley defeats Fil.
Stanley doesn't defeat Gary,
who is named for her grandmother,
whose bejeweled given name
of "Garnet" is shortened to "Gary"
to make other people's lives
a little easier. Gary tells us

that she is a bartender.

She is taciturn and serious,
down to her wire-rimmed glasses,
while Fil wears a scarf tied
vaguely like a bow tie, and
Stanley, a bespectacled woman
with an easy laugh, thinks
slowly and carefully before
she responds to the host's
silly, scripted questions.

On the day I read an article
describing our nation's
marshmallow-minded president
signing a bill rescinding
measures to bridge the gender gap
in payrolls, I watch
on subscription TV
as smiling celebrities
and ordinary people
in wide-lapelled jackets
and polyester headbands
try to match their answers
to comedic fill-in-the-blanks.
There are the requisite jokes
about brainless, big-busted women
and men with shrewish wives
whom they wish they could trade
for gleaming Maseratis.

Gary is defeated
eventually, of course,
though the rerun series
never shows that episode.
In the meantime she loses

every chance she gets
to win the jackpot rounds.

The word "jackpot"
was first used in the years
just after the Civil War.
It comes from a game
of poker that centers
on the jack, that wily knave,
that smooth-tongued bad boy,
who keeps one hidden eye
on the queen's red-robed body,
the other on the power
he cradles in his pocket,
a power he worries
she might—if she sets
her mind to it—steal,
along with his name.

CRAVING

I can hear wise mothers
say it is the body's way
of crying out for what it lacks,
but there is more to this
than mineral deficiency.

Here the rigid scientist
can deny the soul,
but my bones alone
in their hunger for calcium
don't impel me to rocky road

any more than this animal
determined to project her DNA
accounts for the way I look at him—
his eyes turned and his hair mussed
as daylight slips through shadows.

There is a vibrancy to need,
the heart a perched bird
and the body a taut wire,
weariness and energy entwined,
a reminder we are alive.

Or like this: the fruit hangs
from the laden branch,
just out of reach.
We reach anyway, savoring
this wild electrical stretch.

Walking on Eggshells

What a relief to realize
we can't. How freeing
to hear at that first step
the crunch, to feel in our soles
the soft pricks that tickle
more than hurt. The only
unpleasantness: the viscous
ooze of the yolk, the vicious
vision it conjures of
the small animal of love
crushed beneath our weight,
its golden blood sticking to
our own thickening skin.

Wonder Woman at 90

has lost a bit of her zoom.
No more rescuing
a sinking battleship full
of confused, drowning sailors,
no more squashing
evil overlords like so many
roaches in a hog trough.
No, these days she's happy
pouring water over thirsty tulips,
lounging in bubble baths,
sipping tea every afternoon,
incognito, with Catwoman,
who, it turns out, isn't the bitch
that liar Batman always
insisted. But don't be deceived:
she's still Wonder Woman. She
still keeps her bright eyes open.
Just ask the cruel fool
leering through the chain links
at kindergarten dodge ball
or the blind date shoving
his brogan in the doorjamb.
He tells the doctor
that all he can remember
is the flash of silver hair
before the sudden *POW!*—
before the dull crunch
of flimsy bone.

That Hurt

Sometimes in a scalded moment,
someone you love unveils a thing
that has lain long silent between you,
some ancient pain or betrayal,
real or imagined, your fault or the beloved's
or neither's, but fault doesn't matter,
all that matters is the hurt that now throbs
like a tooth in need of pulling, or the hollow socket,
with a pulse of its own, almost a body of its own
and a soul. You could speak to that hurt,
tell it that it's worn out its welcome, ask it why
it won't leave for good, won't storm from the house
in the midnight rain. No, it lingers,
fingering your favorite mug, turning up the burner
beneath your tea kettle, eyeing your easy chair,
planning to waste the night with stories
you've already told it you don't want to hear.
You're stuck, sad host to this unwelcome boarder.
Even if it gave you half a breath to speak,
there's nothing you could say to chase it off.
Unlike the voice of the one you love,
yours hasn't the power of thunder
to rattle shut doors in the frames
that you thought fit them snugly, but see, now?
                              They're loose,
loose as a furious tongue.

When the Dog Bites

My mother sat in her small rocker,
smoked cigarettes and nodded off
from overtime hours and overcooking
meat too lean for anyone's tastes
to save my father's arteries
as she had saved all else about us.

By 8 p.m. she was off to bed
most nights, habits established
by years of shiftwork, but come the holidays
she'd stay awake to see Perry Como
sing lazily of sleigh bells and drummer boys,
watch Jimmy Stewart delight to find
Zuzu's petals in his watch pocket,
hear Julie Andrews itemize
in clear soprano her favorite things.

She loved the beauty of the Alps she'd never
walked herself but only seen
once a year in gleaming Technicolor,
and she loved the stern kindness of the Reverend Mother,
reminding her of nuns who filled the void
left by the mother she lost. herself, so young
her childhood withered, a leaf on a starved vine.

Always she went to bed before the Nazis—
their sour faces, their crooked-spider stares—
emerged from the darkness to drag the Captain
to join their cruelty crusade, the sort that we
have seen too many times. I would remind her,
year after year, she knew the movie ended

in hope, in escape, the family outfoxing foxes,
the youngest carried on the backs of the oldest
improbably in sunshine and warmth
across the glittering mountains she loved.
"Doesn't matter," she'd say. "I don't want to see Nazis."
She would crush out her cigarette and rise from her chair.

I know now this woman had seen enough cruelties
at men's hands to last fifty Christmases.
I knew as much then, but I didn't understand
why happy endings don't wipe out intermittent
sadness and danger. I would tell myself
she needed her sleep. And maybe she did.

But twenty years after she fell from the cancer
that invaded her lungs, I sit in a house,
warm but not paid for, six counties away
from what's left of our family, worry descending
on all of us like years we have lost
and can never retrieve. Our endings may be
happier than any dreadful present
dares predict, and still we stare down at our hands,
counting scars, faint or giant, from every scrape.

Come morning, back then, I would wake, songs forgotten
in place of the business I'd planned for the day.
My mother, across town, in a nurse's uniform,
checked boxes on forms, offered aspirin to workers,
and sometimes, on bloodier days, pulled dark sutures
through swollen fingers bitten by machines.
The scars her stitches would leave on the hands
of men and women working through this harsh world
would one day, in their healing, leave puckers and swells
that resembled small valleys, minute mountain peaks.

Mothers Build Stories

with words the size of old-growth planks,
of massive bricks shaped smooth and thick
and sharp on edges, all to lift children
to solid ground from slippery pits, to talk them
down, like scared kittens, from high limbs
and ledges, or simply to quiet them
when night settles on its haunches
to rest, to roost like weary hens
in soft nests of fog.

Mother was a master of necessary invention,
the spin of a tale to explain away suspicion,
disappointment, disaster, the frail pain
of failure. My sister, deemed too old
to suck the rubber nipple, was told
the Mama owl in her supple wisdom
flew down in dark and stole away
what an old girl didn't need
to give it to her babies, young and hooting
the livelong day, so the Mama never slept.
My sister hushed her moaning,
suddenly proud, suddenly grown.

When our skeptic selves asked
on the cusp of a bright Christmas
how a fat man would deposit gifts
in a house without a chimney,
Mama pointed to the doorknob,
whispered, "Santa can blink twice,
shrink without a word to the size
of a feather on a hummingbird.
Then he zips through the keyhole, the end
of a thread through the eye of a needle."

What is it worth, this wonder
her words purchased for us?

This woman who read newsprint
and grocery labels mostly,
who worked in a world as practical
as sawdust and red clay.
The air she breathed bulged with smoke.
Dishwater singed her fingers.

And when we whined in our soft privilege
at boredom some summer day,
she handed us shakers, told us in tones
honest as a preacher's that, if we only peppered
a robin's wing, it was sure to let us catch it
in our small, sincere hands. And we believed.

Years later, grown and alone, I watched
a mourning dove trapped in a stairwell,
frantic wings flapping, her bloodied head
pounding the plate glass window that loomed
a gloomy joke above the muddy steps.
Without thinking, I grabbed her, her warm heart
beating a flurry in her purple breast.
Outside, knowing she would die,
I named her baby, held her curled and terrified
in still hands as I imagined a world
where my touch could make a gentle thing
immortal, a story I built before spreading
my fingers like wings, before I let go
of that creature, her doomed and beautiful life.

Leah, Rachel, Dinah

It took the two of them
to make the patriarch whole,
his desire tricked
by another wily father
and the silence of the brides
whose only reward
lay in the sons they would bear.

The prophet explained
how God pitied Leah,
the unwanted, so he gave her
a fertile womb.
But Rachel would give birth
to the son most loved.

Two more women
defined as vessels.
How does Eve's curse become
the only hope of her daughters?

Leah's daughter, Dinah,
appears in the Bible
only to be raped, only to incite
a battle. Another woman
defined as a man's
receptacle, as men's
bloody path to the tomb.

Shouldn't we ask
if Leah wanted Jacob, if
Rachel wanted sons,

if Dinah wanted a self
to call her own?

In this asking
rest the asking
and the answer,
like twins. Like

the bounty
God shall provide
and the thanksgivings
men proclaim.
While the women
rest in shadows, waiting
for their moment
to bless or to curse.

Clinging

Because my room has wide windows
that open to the southern light,
you set out, that November, to bring
your potted perennials to weather the winter
in the bay at the edge of my bed.
My jade, your hawthorn, my jasmine, your purple-
throated hibiscus shared the curved space --
the radiated air, the incandescent light --
I returned to most evenings,
paling from the deepening cold.

On occasions when you visited,
eased enough to slip from your clothes,
thinking I'd passed down the hallway, you spoke
in a quiet voice to every growing thing
that rested there, yours or mine, no matter,
and anyhow, in a long blue season,
the vines and branches had tangled so
they needed each other to tilt toward the light:
siblings joined in a mother's womb,
wondering if they needed to be born.
In shadows, I strained my ears to hear you
whisper your prayers above them:
stay with us, *stay with us*, as if they were children
turning from the house, as if they were prophets
struggling to lay their lives down at last
for distant, capricious gods.

Now, if I could see you,
I would tell you they still live, so many winters
later. Their limbs curl as they reach

nearer the ceiling each day.

In spring, when the window is cracked for the breeze,

air rushes through them, like birdsong, like waves,

like men's hushed voices begging mother spirits:

let us go, let us go, let us go

Neighbors, 2017

We don't know each other's names.
The land we live in deems it wise
to be wary of strangers. Still,
we wave at each other, sometimes,
across this narrow street. You could
open your front door; I could
open mine, and we could gaze—
if the light were right—into each
other's insides, but the weather
suddenly turned cold. It gets
dark too early these days. We leave
our doors shut all the time.
When we venture out, as people
must, our bodies are bundled
in layers of insulated fabric.
One of us could be arrested,
and the other could not pick
the face out of a line-up. We keep
to our designated borders.
But this much I know from the barking:
we both have dogs in our back yards.
In the afternoons, as shadows lengthen,
they quiet down. They settle themselves
in their favorite patches of warmish earth,
nearest our back doors, waiting for us,
out of habit, to let them come in.

PARENTS

Now that they're gone,
I stare in the mirror
searching for his eyes,
her smile, the skin
that brushed against mine,
the skin that held me
inside itself.
Some days I see them
in shades or shadows.
Some days I lose them
in the flash of a pupil,
that small black hole.

Sick with Love

What maniacs we are—sick with love, all of us.
                    --Megan Mayhew Bergman

She understood, the woman who bore me
fifteen years after her youngest, hoping
that mothering another into her old age
would spare her the cure of this illness
she'd nursed herself into her whole life.
A fifteen-year-old girl, she lay in the big bed
on the open edge at night, her left hand brushing
the loaded Crescent, five younger siblings
on her other side breathing hoarsely,
a father gone courting in a distant valley,
a mother sixty miles away, buried in dark clay.

She put me in their places forty years later,
my drunken father pounding on her thin door,
a steak knife in her bedside table drawer,
weariness in her eyes. And when that man
quit his drinking, toned down just a slight
his loudest words, he fell into the hospital,
lungs clotted with blood he might have spilled
had she not held him back, and in her gentle
way of being necessary, she slept
stiffly on a pallet on gray linoleum
beside his electric bed. No one had to tell her
how worry drowned a body like pneumonia,
the disease that killed her mother, and when her own
lungs sprouted deadly flowers, she cursed her child
for speaking to the doctor of cigarettes.

The bed she died in
was narrow, new and made fresh every week,
lined on either side with metal rails
cold to her reddened touch. I imagine,
since no one told me, how she stared between
aluminum bars at shadows in the doorway,

counted in her mind outstanding debts,
overlooked the credits. In love, in school,
I wasn't there. I overlooked how close
she was to letting the world's pale filaments
slip from fingers too weak to grasp a hand.

She did and did not want me to know.
I did and did not want to know.
I wonder what words I might have said.
I know better, and still
often I tell myself she was beyond
hearing words, as if the bars held her complete
and bodiless already, a hologram,
a shape in wildfire burning whitely
enough to kill the pathogen, and more. To blind
sad eyes like lightning, to deafen
pricked ears with thunder like shotgun blasts.

In Dreams

Often in dreams my mother is not dead
but run away, her old silver LeSabre
—unused, unplated now beneath the carport—
gleaming, speeding down highways I've never seen.

Or sometimes she's been away but has come back
for a moment only, a cup of instant coffee,
a gathering of small things, movement toward the doorway,
and I stand pleading. My father sits still.

In dreams like this she's often young and rose-skinned,
a way I never knew her, black-haired, laughing,
never slow or sickly. I ask her to stay
so we can be girls together. She vanishes.

In other dreams she wears unpatterned scarves
around her head. I know then she is dying,
and no one else does. I tell her she must stay
since time is poison. She waves a fading hand.

Sometimes when I wake I open my eyes
and wonder how often she wished before she fell
ill to leave the cracked walls that caged us,
unwashed, unpatched, crumbling to dust behind her.

Sometimes when I wake I keep my eyes closed
and wonder what she would say to me that morning
if she were alive. I hear outside the train songs,
the rush of jet engines, the distant traffic's hum.

Harvest

Each new little loss and
the largest return,
fresh and sharp
as September apples.

Imagine, when another
large loss descends, the
windstorm that shakes
from the reddening trees

a cloudburst of fruit
too bruised and bitter
to be eaten. And still
we must eat.

Replenishing

In bed last night you found the dry patch
in the small of my back and asked if I knew
it was there. I didn't, but I knew what it was.
Not the little desert you called it. Instead,
an inheritance, a purple legacy
from a mother who spent forty-three years
fighting the cracks in her hands,
the scales on her arms that shamed her to wearing
long sleeves in Augusta dog days,
the crust on her scalp thickened by
the astringency of hair spray,
the constriction of nicotine.

A doctor she worked for once insisted
a cure for cancer would spell a cure
for psoriasis. They operate, he explained,
on similar principles, cells reproducing
faster than the body can embrace them.
She banked that nugget of hope. And when
she started the chemo thirteen years later,
her skin shone soft as strawberry cream.
Each day she touched thinned fingertips
to a new, smooth scalp.
"Bald as a baby," she'd say.

Half a year after she died,
you made love to me at last.
In the quiet after, I told you how
she offered a makeshift confession
to my oldest sister. If anyone counts
things left undone as sins.
She spoke of the melons she would not plant
that spring, the quiltscraps unpatched,
a brother not heard from since childhood.
But God, she said, could never hold against her
greed, theft, deceit, adultery.

Dying in a room she'd kept alone
beside my father's for twenty-five years,
she said he was the only man
she'd touched in her life.

You are my fourth. The night I told you
this story, you held me tight as a breath,
offering no stories of your own

and taking no more, your hands outstretching,
full and strong, across my wide hips,
as if I were a child you had to hold back
from racing into dangerous streets.
I loved you for that.
Like I loved you last night,
when, craving your wholeness, I pressed slow fingers
through thick curls on your chest, your belly, your thighs,

reaching for the fresh flesh beneath.

Their Love Story

For my parents

He could not read love poems to her; his eyes
saw the letters darting on the page
to spaces they never belonged, like summer flies
caught inside a window. He was no sage,
no oracle, and she always understood
what he never did. No wonder he felt afraid
that, sensing his stumbling, someday someone would
convince her she was foolish to have stayed
beside him all this time. And he knew
he was lacking elsewhere too. He could be cruel.
Often he worried so that he drank a few,
or more than a few, too many. Still,
how happy he was, when he told her, to hear her say
she never cared much for poetry anyway.

The Ceremony

I dig the hole through field dust,
pale charcoal down to clay like blood.
My father stands in cedar shadows

explaining, again, he is seventy-six
years old. I know this acre as well
as I know my own breath. A rough-kneed girl

in cotton skirts hid among cornrows,
outwitting boy cousins, loving the uncle
who grew Silver Queen and gave away quarters

twenty-five years ago, who died
slowly a month past my eighteenth birthday,
infection in the blood. What killed

my sister's cat, the one named Smoke
for his dusky shade of fur, none of us alive
will know. His thin body waits

at the edge of the woods, some fifteen steps
from where my father stands. My sister,
inside the house, has supper to cook,

a bad back to nurse. He tells me
he bets it will rain tonight, then begins
to tell Rover's story as if it were new.

His prize German shepherd, nineteen years old,
who couldn't walk at last. Five dollars
to have him put down. Five more to the man

who buried him fifty yards from the spot
where I dig right now. The shady side of the field.
I remember that night at the dinner table

twenty-five years ago. How my father
ate more than I thought he would. He told
us girls that, when the time came, he wanted

to be buried in bedsheets beside his old dog.
Less cost, he said. Mama didn't laugh.
We stared back at our black-eyed peas.

Today, he knows better than we do
the letters of his name and date of his birth
have already darkened in the burnished stone

just to the left of Mama's name and dates.
He cried in his hands the night her lungs gave up,
told her they would meet in better places,

then lifted her untouched dinner plate
and left the room to my sister. So I was told.
A month later, I drove him to buy the slate

marker he called the color of earth.
I say nothing of any of this
as I cover Smoke with the land my father's

father bought sixty years ago.
I listen to his voice one last time
apologize for weakness, for his old age.

I drop the shovel. He chuckles, asks,

"Should we offer a prayer?" I bend and slap
my hands to knock the dust away.

From a distance, we look like tricksters sharing
a belly-deep joke, or else I might seem
a silly adult snatching at fireflies

flitting through duskglow, just out of reach.

CALHOUN

On this street where once nine people
bowed in prayer were shot to death
by an average madman,
a child walks a puddled sidewalk
three steps behind her mother.

In her path, a crippled wren
splutters half-winged, uncertain
what to do if not fly.
The child lifts to her chest
this weary casualty
of a summer storm it had
no part in building. The mother,
hearing her child's cries,
takes the bird in one hand,
the child's hand in the other,
takes charge as if she knows
exactly what to do.

None of us behind them can know
exactly what she'll do,
but we can imagine kindness.
We can imagine nurturance,
rejuvenation. In this small world,
boiled in its antique acids,
such scenes unfold before us
just often enough to make us wonder
if perhaps, in fact, there's love.

CAIM

A sanctuary, on the one hand. A mystic circle
of protection spun around the Celtic pilgrim
by his own hand, and by the hymn that shoots
from his plaintive throat. A demon, on the other,
the murderous brother doomed to roam the earth
including, no doubt, the green Irish hills
where the natives spoke his name to rhyme with *time*.

I stumble on this word on this day
when my sister in her prison of locked joints
lies in her bed two hours away, no more
or less afraid than usual, a day when I
discover a friend I've mostly known through e-mail
and traded poems has suffered a massive stroke
and soon will die when someone flips a switch.
My heart of late has been too slow to beat,
and that both is and isn't a metaphor,
so wires taped to my skin track its movements,
my weary criminal under house arrest.

Outside, the summer solstice air is dry
and cooler than usual. I step on the front porch
and look at flowers planted in March and April—
petunia, torenia, dahlia, marigold—
in pots that line the path and climb the steps.
The summer is not yet strong enough
to scorch their lightest petals, but given time
it will be. I pour cool water over bloom
and leaf and soil. With a cotton cloth I wipe
the rim of every lush pot. I whisper
the names of people I love but cannot save.
Perhaps it's prayer enough to an antique god
to keep at least the flowers healthy for now.
Perhaps it's not, but sometimes we can do
no more in this dusky world than plead to air.

VISITATION

In my hands silk flowers
the colors of November,
rich and dark as
my mother loved,
and I begin to bend
in late afternoon gold
warmer than the season
should allow.
The cemetery is bright
and quiet. Until
the wind rises, and I hear
a rush behind me.
I turn my head,
straighten my back,
stare at the wild pear tree,
leaves the color of flame.
It shivers in wind,
blazes billowing. Still
I stare. I don't move.

I think of Moses listening
to the voice of God.
In Sunday school the teachers
read it slow and thundering,
a chastening bluster,
the angry father insisting
his children bow and scrape.
Perhaps it was instead
this tender whisper.
Perhaps it was instead
the hushed singing
of our mothers, their breath
tousling our hair,
their voices falling
around our weary shoulders like
manna, like sunlight.

The Thought of Losing You

stiffens me.

I am a fallen
tree petrified
in seconds, not
centuries.

I am a bird
running (not
flying), crushed
between avalanche
and sandstone, my bones
cross-stitching strata
of pre-history.
What use
are slow wings?

Looking back
at our chain-linked
lives, I become
Lot's wife, but harder:
granite the bleached
white of table salt.

How much better
to be the blackened
timber of the jetty,
the last surface
to hold you
before whatever grows
inside you

compels you
to dive.

Elegy for Elegies

I am done with the names
of lonely things.

Tired too of Jesus
and guilt, that gloomy duo
reminding us of what
is always lost.

Everywhere an absence,
bright blossoms whose brilliance
dulls in new sun.

Let now be.

Declare the cotton
falling from cottonwood
a giving, not a leaving.

Touch the rosemary and lift
fingertips to your nose. Gawk
at stiff phalluses of pine trees
shaking their sex
in your face.

In the garden, an apple,
missing one bite.

Further Reading

by
Tiffany Woodley

1.   *A Dangerous Heaven* serves as both a piece and the title of this collection. Explore the way the title speaks to the poems within. How does the full poem embellish that meaning?

2.   Throughout this collection, Edwins explores varied themes and ideas that are each poignant. Which poems took hold of you? Which have you chosen to carry?

3.   Poems such as "Clinging" and "Wonder Woman at 90" shift between action and inaction yet do so in different ways. How does Edwins establish and balance this turn in her poems?

4.   Many of the pieces in this volume examine moments from the Bible through a feminist lens including "Eve", "Leah, Rachel, Dinah", "Mary"; and "Magdalene". How does the author's retelling of these stories alter your thoughts on these classic tales?

5.   Edwins uses details from news sources as an entryway into "This Year", "From Wire Reports", "Miniature Coffins" and "The Children Have Stopped Crying". What do these tell you about the speaker's relationship with the world? How does what captures her attention develop her larger perspectives?

6.   "The Concept of Order" and "For Newtown, For Townville" wrestle with the heavy weight of large-scale tragedy. In contrast, "The Thought of Losing You" and "The Ceremony" (among others) focus on personal loss. In what ways does the author navigate these distinct types of loss? How does she use style to make them similar? different?

7.   There are a number of topics that feel like odd pairings: David Bowie and sewage pipes; nursery rhymes and school shootings; The Sound of Music and a nurse's trail of scars are only a few. How does bringing these seemingly disjointed elements together create a unified message in the poems?

8.   "Like" speaks to the inadequacy of similarity, yet one highlight of this book appears in the author's ability to elevate meaning through comparison. She speaks of a mother's ability to calm children by "talk[ing] them / down, like scared kittens, from high limbs"; refers to an older woman's face "as beautiful / as a stopped heart" and a church's walls "thick as history"; God resting in "a bed / softer than forgiveness" and the way our brains lead us to incorrect conclusions "faster / than the rickety heel / on a cheap pair of pumps". How do these comparisons create new meanings?

9. As Edwins explores the nature of humanity, she also explores our connections with neighbors, mothers, fathers, lovers, and even a stranger in a cafe. Where does she place tensions and where are connections more peaceful? Why?

10. Complexity is infused into objects throughout the work which serve to illuminate human aspects. For instance, the poet uses an MRI machine as a gateway to a memento mori (reminder of the inevitability of death). Which objects stand out as holding or triggering layered emotions?

11. Edwins pays homage to the practice of storytelling in her work through references to nursery rhymes, comic books, old wives tales, biblical figures & family folklore. Which stories feel most familiar? How does her use of allusion add to the meaning of the poems where they are referenced? What part does storytelling play in our humanity?

12. Though most of the poems here are written in free verse, there are two villanelles and a sonnet. Villanelles contain repetition which builds to the climactic final stanza and sonnets often probe a specific topic, like love. Go back to "Breaking News", "Miniature Coffins" and "Their Love Story" and dissect the relationship between the structure of these poems and their content.

13.   One of the most subtle weapons in this poet's arsenal is her diction. There are many moments that make a reader pause in their reading, words ricocheting and wounding. A few of these occur when she speaks of the "beautifully flawed/world" (1), brothers as "the first tipsy domino" (5), "silence, that valuable/terror" (12), a shoe's "bumble-tongued mate" (32) and the hurt of a "scalded moment" (59). Consider the meanings of these phrases on their own, then go back to their poems and see how their meanings shine in context.

14.   As Edwins navigates a wide array of relationships, she often centers power dynamics: those who hold power and those who lack this privilege. Examine some of the moments where she highlights the responsibility of power such as in "Distances", "Bathsheba" and "A Woman Named Stanley". What is she saying about the responsibility of power? Do her subjects meet its needs?

Acknowledgments

Adanna: A Literary Journal "An American Woman Steps inside an 800-Year-Old Church"
As It Ought to Be Magazine "How It Feels to Be Bodiless"
Autumn Sky Poetry Daily "Visitation"
Calyx "Old Wives' Tale"
The Coil "A Student Spells 'Abel' as 'Able'"
Cordella Magazine "The Ceremony" and "Sick with Love"
descant "Magdalene"
Fall Lines "Like"
Hunnybee "Neighbors, 2017"
The Literary Nest "The Bedouin Wife" and "Postcard"
Mom Egg Review "Eve"
Naugatuck River Review "Replenishing"
Number One "Walking around Furniture"
Ocotillo Review "For Newtown, For Townville"
Old Red Kimono "In Dreams"
Parentheses Journal "The Beauty of Stark Things"
Poetry Super Highway "A Failure of Seeing" and "This Year"
Red Rock Review "Geophagy"
Redheaded Stepchild "Actias Luna"
Right Hand Pointing "Parents"
Rise Up Review "Miniature Coffins" and "Wonder Woman at 90"
Rockvale Review "Appellations"
Rogue Agent "MRI"
Sojourn: A Journal of the Arts "Clinging" and "Her Cap"
Thimble Literary Magazine "Mary"
Whale Road Review "The Children Have Stopped Crying"
The Write Launch "The Concept of Order" and "That Hurt"
Zone 3 "Coordinates" and "The Last Wild Elephant Alive"
"Craving" originally appeared in *The Way to My Heart: An Anthology of Food-Related Romance*, ed. Kelly Ann Jacobson.

The epigraph to "A Failure of Seeing" is quoted from Matt Haig's *The Humans* (Simon & Schuster, 2013).

The epigraph to "Sick with Love" is quoted from Meghan Mayhew Bergman's "Housewifely Arts," from *Birds of a Lesser Paradise* (Scribner, 2012).

Personal Acknowledgements

Since this is a first full-length book by a writer in her fifties, the poems in this collection were written over a span of some twenty-plus years. Some of the people who helped me in one way or another to complete this collection are people I've not seen or spoken to in over a decade, and some helpers have passed away. Also, I have an almost crippling fear that I will omit unintentionally a name, and I will immediately regret that omission when I finally see this book in print. If you fall into that category, please forgive me—I will announce you from the hilltops every chance (and at every reading) from now through eternity.

Let me begin by thanking the two folks who read the manuscript in full and gave encouragement and feedback prior to its publication—my dear friends Kristin Robertson and Marcella Fleischman Pixley, both amazing writers themselves (go out and read their books). I've known you both since the last century, as our students love to say, and I will always adore you and be your cheerleaders! My mentor in graduate school and friend in life and in poetry since then, Marilyn Kallet, deserves at least the same level of praise and good wishes that she has always given me, and in ways she doesn't know, she was instrumental in the shaping of some of the poems in this book. I know for certain that at least one of the poems in this book was workshopped in an informal poetry writing group I was a part of years ago in Knoxville that included Kristin Robertson, Curt Rode, and Louise Mosrie Coombe. They made up the first group of poets I worked with regularly to whom I felt truly connected, and I thank you all for that experience.

My three closest friends in particular have provided poem praise and emotional support over the years: Misty McGinnis Bailey, Amanda Wilkerson Lawrence, and Dollie Newhouse. I really don't know where I'd be without the three of you, and I cannot thank you all enough for that. You all are like sisters to me, and my only regret is that we don't live in the same city so I can see you all more often! Various treasured friends and sounding boards over the years of working on this manuscript deserve praise: Dinah

Brock, Adam and Landon Houle, Christopher D. Johnson, Shel Veenstra Johnson, Natalie Mahaffey, Christine Masters-Wheeler, Sara Melton, Dawn Larsen, Meredith Love, Meredith Reynolds, Laura Rutland, Deloris Samuel, Jennifer V. Stowe, Cheryl Tuttle, Lance Weldy, and Nancy Zaice. Jon Tuttle has been one of my biggest professional cheerleaders over the last nineteen years, and I will always be grateful for that (plus we bond over cat worship). I must give a shout-out to friends Michael Budd and Tom Mack, who always are eager to share drinks and good food when I visit my home stomping grounds of the Aiken/Augusta area. Tom also has supported my work as a poet and as a fellow board member on two state boards we've served on over the last decade, SC Humanities and the South Carolina Academy of Authors. I also thank members and staff of both of those boards for being powerful advocates for the arts and humanities in South Carolina. Thanks also to Leah Maines and the folks at Finishing Line Press for publishing my first in-print collection, my chapbook Play, in 2016 (longtime friend Jean Gordon Phelps did the wonderful cover art for that book, and our mutual longtime friend Angie Attaway always cheers me on as her "favorite liberal"). And of course, the wonderful folks at Gnashing Teeth Publishing deserve the highest praise for taking a chance on this manuscript, which had been floating around since 2018 seeking a publisher. Thank you, Karen Cline-Tardiff and the wonderful staff at Gnashing Teeth. It feels great to be a Gnasher!

This book would not have come together were it not for a sabbatical and two summer research stipends I received from Francis Marion University prior to its compilation as a manuscript. In 2019, FMU President Fred Carter chose me to be a Trustees Research Scholar for the university, which each year thereafter provided time and financial support to tweak elements of the manuscript, originally assembled in 2018. Before I became a board member, the South Carolina Academy of Authors awarded me the 2014 Carrie McCray Nickens fellowship, which provided encouragement and some monetary support. I am also grateful to countless conference organizers who supported my work by inviting me to read poems at those conferences, especially the PCA/ACA Creative Writing division (headed by the absolutely fabulous Katie Manning) and the PCAS/ACAS conference organizers. Some of the poets I've met at these conferences have become long-distance friends who have provided necessary "virtual" support over the years (here is where I'm sure I will regretfully forget some names). Let me give a shout-out to Katie Manning again as well as to Sally Rosen Kindred, David Oates, Mary Buchinger Bodwell, Karen Bjork Kubin, Lindsay Illich, Nat O'Reilly, and Sarah Ann Winn. Also, to W.M. Epes, Christine Klocek-Lim, and Clif Mason, thanks so much for all the online support of mine and others' poetry that you provide!

My students always are major inspirations. There have been thousands of them by now. They don't all remember me, and given the way my poor mind works, I don't remember all their names. But they were always the audience I fretted over most, even though the words I shared with them usually weren't from my own poetry. Some have become longtime friends. Of course I can't possibly name all the students who made a big difference for me—I have to trust they know who they are. But one in particular I must name is middle-grades novelist Allison Varnes, who has remained in contact with me for some twenty-odd years and has often exchanged writer stories with me over the years. She has made a point always to be thankful to me in her own book acknowledgments, which has meant more than she could know. I also want to thank Amanda Lawrence and Tanya Long Bennett for inviting me as a featured poet to their campuses, where I got to interact with even more students than those in my classes.

Friends who are gone now: Deborah Scaperoth and Susan Laughter Meyers—you were always supportive souls, and you sent kind words or exchanged poems for discussion via the internet. Your spirits continue to shine brightly to all who knew you. William B. Larsen—you were an inspiration in a thousand ways, and I'm still writing poems about you.

To my family—I could not have been who I am without you. Every book I ever publish will be dedicated in some way to my late parents, Joe O. and Beatrice McCarty Edwins. My sister Sandra Edwins, like our dad before her, loves to brag on me embarrassingly to others, and her help and love from various directions over the years was enormous. My sister Linda Edwins Bishop happily cheers me on when I get anything published, and my niece and nephew Shanna Mullis Hood and Brandon Mullis will always be dear to me and always bring joy when I'm with them. Thanks too to Brandon for the magnificent cover art for this book! Great-nephews Corey and Cameron Gamache—never underestimate the power of your creativity.

Finally, thanks to anyone reading this volume (and especially those who have read this far). We often fail to appreciate the power of words, but what continually astonishes me is that anyone chooses to embrace the words I put together, even though I often don't quite know how or why. Let us all encourage others to read widely, and let us all fight to preserve everyone's freedom to choose what to read.

About the Author

Jo Angela Edwins has published poems in over 100 journals, including *Calyx*, *New South*, *Zone 3*, *The Hollins Critic*, and *Mom Egg Review*. Her chapbook **Play** was published in 2016 by Finishing Line Press. She has received awards from Winning Writers, Poetry Super Highway, and the South Carolina Academy of Authors and is a Pushcart Prize, Forward Prize, and Bettering American Poetry nominee. She lives in Florence, SC, where she teaches at Francis Marion University and serves as the first poet laureate of the Pee Dee region of South Carolina.

Printed in the USA
CPSIA information can be obtained
at www.ICGtesting.com
LVHW041042241124
797241LV00007B/779